The

PRAYER

of

JABEZ

Oh that you would bless me indeed!

CHARLES H. SPURGEON

Table of Contents

Introduction

Sowing in Tears, Reaping in Joy

We know very little about Jabez, except that he was more honorable than his brethren, and that he was called Jabez because his mother bore him with sorrow. It will sometimes happen that where there is the most sorrow in the antecedents, there will be the most pleasure in the sequel. As the furious storm gives place to the clear sunshine, so the night of weeping precedes the morning of joy. Sorrow the harbinger; gladness the prince it ushers in. Cowper says:

"The path of sorrow, and that path alone,
Leads to the place where sorrow is unknown."

To a great extent we find that we must sow in tears before we can reap in joy. Many of our works for Christ have cost us tears. Difficulties and disappointments have wrung our soul with anguish. Yet those projects that have cost us more than ordinary sorrow, have often turned out to be the most honorable of our undertakings. While our grief called the offspring of desire "Benoni," the son of my sorrow, our faith has been afterwards able to give it a name of delight, "Benjamin," the son of my right hand.

You may expect a blessing in serving God if you are enabled to persevere under many discouragements. The ship is often long coming home, because detained on the road by excess of cargo. Expect her freight to be the better when she reaches the port.

A Man of Prayer More honorable than his brethren was the child whom his mother bore with sorrow. As for this Jabez, whose aim was so well pointed, his fame so far sounded, his name so lastingly embalmed; he was a man of prayer. The honor he enjoyed would not have been worth having if it had not been vigorously contested and equitably won. His devotion was the key to his promotion. Those are the best honors that come from God, the award of grace with the acknowledgment of service. When Jacob was surnamed Israel, he received his princedom after a memorable night of prayer. Surely it was far more honorable to him than if it had been bestowed upon him as a flattering distinction by some earthly emperor. The best honor is that which a man gains in communion with the Most High.

Jabez, we are told, was more honorable than his brethren, and his prayer is forthwith recorded, as if to intimate that he was also more prayerful than his brethren.

The Prayer Itself

We are told of what petitions his prayer consisted. All through it was very significant and instructive. We have only time to take one clause of it; indeed, that one clause may be said to comprehend the rest: "Oh that you would bless me indeed!" I commend it as a prayer for yourselves, dear brethren and sisters; one which will be available at all seasons; a prayer to begin Christian life with, a prayer to end it with, a prayer which would never be unseasonable in your joys or in your sorrows.

"Indeed" – true vs. false blessings

Oh that you, the God of Israel, the covenant God, would bless me indeed! The very pith of the prayer seems to lie in that word, "indeed." There are many varieties of blessing. Some are blessings only in name: they gratify our wishes for a moment, but permanently disappoint our expectations. They charm the eye, but pall on the taste. Others are mere temporary blessings: they perish with the using. Though for awhile they regale the senses, they cannot satisfy the higher cravings of the soul. But, "Oh that you would bless me indeed!"

"Thou" – what are true blessings

I know whom God blesses shall be blessed. The thing good in itself is bestowed with the good-will of the giver, and shall be productive of so much good fortune to the recipient that it may well be esteemed as a blessing "indeed," for there is nothing comparable to it.

Let the grace of God prompt it, let the choice of God appoint it, let the bounty of God confer it, and then the endowment shall be something godlike indeed; something worthy of the lips that pronounce the benediction, and verily to be craved by every one who seeks honor that is substantial and enduring. "Oh that you would bless me indeed!" Think it over, and you will see that there is a depth of meaning in the expression.

"Bless" – God's vs. men's blessings

We may set this in contrast with human blessings: "Oh that you would bless me indeed!" It is very delightful to be blessed by our parents, and those venerable friends whose benedictions come from their hearts, and are backed up by their prayers. Many a poor man has had no other legacy to leave his children except his blessing, but the blessing of an honest, holy, Christian father is a rich treasure to his son. One might well feel it were a thing to be deplored through life if he had lost a parent's blessing. We like to have it. The blessing of our spiritual parents is consolatory. Though we believe in no priest-craft, we like to live in the affections of those who were the means of bringing us to Christ, and from whose lips we were instructed in the things of God.

And how very precious is the blessing of the poor! I do not wonder that Job treasured that up as a sweet thing. "When the ear heard me, then it blessed me." If you have relieved the widow and the fatherless, and their thanks are returned to you in benediction, it is no mean reward.
But, dear friends, after all; all that parents, relatives, saints, and grateful people can do in the way of blessing, falls very far short of what we desire to have. O Lord, we would have the blessings of our fellow-creatures, the blessings that come from their hearts; but, "Oh that You would bless me indeed!" for you can bless with authority. Their blessings may be but words, but yours are effectual. They may often wish what they cannot do, and desire to give what they have not at their own disposal, but your will is omnipotent. You did create the world with but a word. O that such omnipotence would now bespeak me your blessing! Other blessings may bring us some tiny cheer, but in your favor is life. Other blessings are mere tittles in comparison with your blessing; for your blessing is the title "to an inheritance incorruptible"(1 Peter 1:4) and unfading, to "a kingdom which cannot be moved."(Heb. 12:28).

Well therefore might David pray in another place, "With your blessing let the house of your servant be blessed forever."(2 Sam. 7:29).

CHAPTER 1
God's Blessings vs. Men's Blessings

Perhaps in this place, Jabez may have put the blessing of God in contrast with the blessings of men. Men will bless you when you do well for yourself. They will praise the man who is successful in business. Nothing succeeds like success. Nothing has so much the approval of the general public as a man's prosperity. Alas! they do not weigh men's actions in the balances of the sanctuary, but in quite other scales.

You will find those about you who will commend you if you are prosperous; or like Job's comforters, condemn you if you suffer adversity. Perhaps there may be some feature about their blessings that may please you, because you feel you deserve them. They commend you for your patriotism: you have been a patriot. They commend you for your generosity: you know you have been self-sacrificing. Well, but after all, what is there in the verdict of man?

At a trial, the verdict of the policeman who stands in the court, or of the spectators who sit in the court-house, amounts to just nothing. The man who is being tried feels that the only thing that is of importance at all will be the verdict of the jury, and the sentence of the judge. So it will little avail us whatever we may do, how others commend or censure. Their blessings are not of any great value.

But, "Oh that you would bless me," that you would say, "Well done, good and faithful servant."(Matt. 25:23) Commend the feeble service that through your grace my heart has rendered. That will be to bless me indeed.

Flattery
Men are sometimes blessed in a very fulsome sense by flattery. There are always those who, like the fox in the fable, hope to gain the cheese by praising the crow. They never saw such plumage, and no voice could be so sweet as yours. The whole of their mind is set, not on you, but on what they are to gain by you. The race of flatterers is never extinct, though the flattered usually flatter themselves it is so. They may conceive that men flatter others, but all is so palpable and transparent when heaped upon themselves, that

they accept it with a great deal of self-complacency, as being perhaps a little exaggerated, but after all exceedingly near the truth.

We are not very apt to take a large discount off the praises that others offer us; yet, were we wise, we should press to our bosom those who censure us; and we should always keep at arm's length those who praise us, for those who censure us to our face cannot possibly be making a market of us; but with regard to those who extol us, rising early, and using loud sentences of praise, we may suspect, and we shall very seldom be unjust in the suspicion, that there is some other motive in the praise which they render to us than that which appears on the surface.

Young man, are you placed in a position where God honors you? Beware of flatterers. Or have you come into a large estate? Have you abundance? There are always flies where there is honey. Beware of flattery. Young woman, are you fair to look upon? There will be those about you that will have their designs, perhaps their evil designs, in lauding your beauty. Beware of flatterers. Turn aside from all these who have honey on their tongue, because of the poison of asps that is under it. Bethink you of Solomon's caution, "meddle not with him that flatters with his lips."(Prov. 20:19).

Cry to God, "Deliver me from all this vain adulation, which nauseates my soul." So shall you pray to him the more fervently... "Oh that you would bless me indeed!" Let me have your benediction, which never says more than it means; which never gives less than it promises.

If you take then the prayer of Jabez as being put in contrast with the benedictions which come from men, you see much force in it.

CHAPTER 2
God's Blessings vs. Temporal Blessings

But we may put it in another light, and compare the blessing Jabez craved with those blessings that are temporal and transient. There are many bounties given to us mercifully by God for which we are bound to be very grateful; but we must not set too much store by them. We may accept them with gratitude, but we must not make them our idols. When we have them we have great need to cry... "Oh that you would bless me indeed, and make these inferior blessings real blessings;" and if we have them not, we should with greater vehemence cry... Oh that we may be rich in faith, and if not blessed with these external favors, may we be blessed spiritually, and then we shall be blessed indeed."

Wealth

Let us review some of these mercies, and just say a word or two about them. One of the first cravings of men's hearts is wealth. So universal the desire to gain it, that we might almost say it is a natural instinct. How many have thought if they once possessed it they should be blessed indeed! But there are ten thousand proofs that happiness consists not in the abundance which a man possesses. So many instances are well known to you all, that I need not quote any to show that riches are not a blessing indeed. They are rather apparently than really so.

Hence, it has been well said, that when we see how much a man has we envy him; but could we see how little he enjoys we should pity him. Some that have had the most easy circumstances have had the most uneasy minds. Those who have acquired all they could wish, had their wishes been at all sane, have been led by the possession of what they had to be discontented because they had not more.

> *"Thus the base miser starves amid his store,*
> *Broods over his gold, and griping still at more,*
> *Sits sadly pining, and believes he's poor."*

Nothing is more clear to any one who chooses to observe it, than that riches are not the chief good at whose advent sorrow flies, and in whose presence joy perennial springs. Full often wealth cozens the owner. Dainties are spread on his table, but his appetite fails, minstrels wait his bidding, but his ears are deaf to all the strains of music; holidays he may have as many as he pleases, but for him recreation has lost all its charms. Or he is young, fortune has come to him by inheritance, and he makes pleasure his pursuit until sport becomes more irksome than work, and dissipation worse than drudgery.

You know how riches make themselves wings; like the bird that roosted on the tree, they fly away. In sickness and despondency these ample means that once seemed to whisper, "Soul, take your ease,"(Luke 12:19) prove themselves to be poor comforters. In death they even tend to make the pang of separation more acute, because there is the more to leave, the more to lose.

We may well say, if we have wealth, "My God, do not put me with these husks; let me never make a god of the silver and the gold, the goods and the chattels, the estates and investments, which in your providence you have given me. I beseech you, bless me indeed. As for these worldly possessions, they will be my bane unless I have your grace with them."

And if you have not wealth, and perhaps the most of you will never have it, say, "My Father, you have denied me this outward and seeming good, enrich me with your love, give me the gold of your favor, bless me indeed; then allot to others whatever you will, you shall divide my portion, my soul shall wait your daily will; do bless me indeed, and I shall be content."

Fame

Another transient blessing which our poor humanity fondly covets and eagerly pursues is fame. In this respect we would sincerely be more honorable than our brethren, and outstrip all our competitors. It seems natural to us all to wish to make a name, and gain some note in the circle we move in at any rate, and we wish to make that circle wider if we can.

But here, as of riches, it is indisputable that the greatest fame does not bring with it any equal measure of gratification. Men, in seeking after notoriety or honor, have a degree of pleasure in the search which they do not always possess when they have gained their object. Some of the most famous men have also been the most wretched of the human race.

If you have honor and fame, accept it; but let this prayer go up, "My God, you bless me indeed, for what profit were it, if my name were in a thousand mouths, if you should spue it out of your mouth? What matter, though my name were written on marble, if it were not written in the Lamb's Book of Life? These blessings are only apparent blessings, windy blessings, blessings that mock me. Give me your blessing: then the honor which comes of you will make me blessed indeed."

If you happen to have lived in obscurity, and have never entered the lists for honors among your fellow-men, be content to run well your own course and fulfill truly your own vocation. To lack fame is not the most grievous of ills; it is worse to have it like the snow, that whitens the ground in the morning, and disappears in the heat of the day. What does it matter to a dead man that men are talking of him? Get the blessing indeed.

Health

There is another temporal blessing which wise men desire, and legitimately may wish for rather than the other two; the blessing of health. Can we ever prize it sufficiently? To trifle with such a boon is the madness of folly. The highest eulogiums that can be passed on health would not be extravagant. He that has a healthy body is infinitely more blessed than he who is sickly, whatever his estates may be.

Yet if I have health, my bones well set, and my muscles well strung, if I scarcely know an ache or pain, but can rise in the morning, and with elastic step go forth to labor, and cast myself upon my couch at night, and sleep the sleep of the happy, yet, oh let me not glory in my strength! In a moment it may fail me. A few short weeks may reduce the strong man to a skeleton. Consumption may set in, the cheek may pale with the shadow of death. Let not the strong man glory in his strength. The Lord "delights not in the strength of the horse: he takes not pleasure in the legs of a man." (Psalm 147:10). And let us not make our boast concerning these things. Say, you that are in good health...

"My God, bless me indeed. Give me the healthy soul. Heal me of my spiritual diseases. Jehovah Rophi come, and purge out the leprosy that is in my heart by nature: make me healthy in the heavenly sense, that I may not be put aside among the unclean, but allowed to stand among the congregation of your saints. Bless my bodily health to me that I may use it rightly, spending the strength I have in your service and to your glory; otherwise, though blessed with health, I may not be blessed indeed."

Some of you, dear friends, do not possess the great treasure of health. Wearisome days and nights are appointed you. Your bones are become an almanac, in which you note the changes of the weather. There is much about you that is fitted to excite pity. But I pray that you may have the blessing indeed, and I know what that is.

I can heartily sympathize with a sister who said to me the other day, "I had such nearness to God when I was sick, such full assurance, and such joy in the Lord, and I regret to say I have lost it now; that I could almost wish to be ill again, if thereby I might have a renewal of communion with God."

I have oftentimes looked gratefully back to my sick chamber. I am certain that I never did grow in grace one half so much anywhere as I have upon the bed of pain. It ought not to be so. Our joyous mercies ought to be great fertilizers to our spirit; but frequently our griefs are more salutary than our joys. The pruning knife is best for some of us.

Well, after all, whatever you have to suffer, of weakness, of debility, of pain, and anguish, may it be so attended with the divine presence, that this light affliction may work out for you a "far more exceeding and eternal weight of glory" (2 Cor. 4:17), and so you may be blessed indeed.

Home

I will only dwell upon one more temporal mercy, which is very precious; I mean the blessing of home. I do not think any one can ever prize it too highly, or speak too well of it. What a blessing it is to have the fireside, and the dear relationships that gather round the word "Home" -wife, children, father, brother, sister! Why, there are no songs in any language that are more full of music than those dedicated to "Mother." We hear a great deal about the German "Fatherland"; we like the sound. But the word, "Father," is the whole of it. The "land" is nothing: the "Father" is key to the music.

There are many of us, I hope, blessed with a great many of these relationships. Do not let us be content to solace our souls with ties that must before long be sundered. Let us ask that over and above them may come the blessing indeed...

I thank you, my God, for my earthly father; but oh, you be my Father, then am I blessed indeed. I thank you, my God, for a mother's love; but comfort my soul as one whom a mother comforts, then am I blessed indeed. I thank you, Savior, for the marriage bond; but you be the bridegroom of my soul. I thank you for the tie of brotherhood; but you be my brother born for adversity, bone of my bone, and flesh of my flesh. The home you have given me I prize, and thank you for it; but I would dwell in the house of the Lord forever, and be a child that never wanders, wherever my feet may travel, from my Father's house with its many mansions.

You can thus be blessed indeed. If not domiciled under the paternal care of the Almighty, even the blessing of home, with all its sweet familiar comforts, does not reach to the benediction which Jabez desired for himself.

But do I speak to any here that are separated from kith and kin? I know some of you have left behind you in the bivouac of life graves where parts of your heart are buried, and that which remains is bleeding with just so many wounds. Ah, well! the Lord bless you indeed! Widow, your maker is your husband. Fatherless one, he has said, "I will not leave you comfortless: I will come to you." Oh, to find all your relationships made up in him, then you will be blessed indeed!

I have perhaps taken too long a time in mentioning these temporary blessings, so let me set the text in another light. I trust we have had human blessings and temporary blessings, to fill our hearts with gladness, but not to foul our hearts with worldliness, or to distract our attention from the things that belong to our everlasting welfare.

CHAPTER 3
God's Blessings vs. Imaginary Blessings

Let us proceed, thirdly, to speak of imaginary blessings. There are such in the world. From them may God deliver us. "Oh that you would bless me indeed!"

Imaginary blessings to the unsaved

Self-righteousness— Take the Pharisee. He stood in the Lord's house, and he thought he had the Lord's blessing, and it made him very bold, and he spoke with unctuous self-complacency, "God, I thank you, that I am not as other men are," and so on. He had the blessing, and well indeed he supposed himself to have merited it. He had fasted twice in the week, paid tithes of all that he possessed, even to the odd farthing on the mint, and the extra half penny on the cummin he had used. He felt he had done everything. His the blessing of a quiet or a quiescent conscience; good, easy man. He was a pattern to the parish. It was a pity everybody did not live as he did; if they had, they would not have needed any police. Pilate might have dismissed his guards, and Herod his soldiers. He was just one of the most excellent people that ever breathed. He adored the city of which he was a burgess!

Ay; but he was not blessed indeed. This was all his own overweening conceit. He was a mere wind-bag, nothing more and the blessing which he fancied had fallen upon him, had never come. The poor publican whom he thought accursed, went to his home justified rather than he. The blessing had not fallen on the man who thought he had it.

Oh, let every one of us here feel the sting of this rebuke, and pray... "Great God, save us from imputing to ourselves a righteousness which we do not possess. Save us from wrapping ourselves up in our own rags, and fancying we have put on the wedding garments. Bless me indeed. Let me have the true righteousness. Let me have the true worthiness which you can accept, even that which is of faith in Jesus Christ."

False assurance— Another form of this imaginary blessing is found in people who would scorn to be thought self-righteous. Their delusion, however, is near akin. I hear them singing...

"I do believe, I will believe That Jesus died for me, And on his cross he shed his blood, From sin to set me free."

You believe it, you say. Well, but how do you know? Upon what authority do you make so sure? Who told you? "Oh, I believe it." Yes, but we must mind what we believe. Have you any clear evidence of a special interest in the blood of Jesus? Can you give any spiritual reasons for believing that Christ has set you free from sin? I am afraid that some have got a hope that has not got any ground, like an anchor without any fluke; nothing to grasp, nothing to lay hold upon. They say they are saved, and they stick to it they are, and think it wicked to doubt it; but yet they have no reason to warrant their confidence.

When the sons of Kohath carried the ark, and touched it with their hands, they did rightly (Num. 4:4-6,15); but when Uzzah touched it he died (2 Sam. 6:6-7). There are those who are ready to be fully assured; there are others to whom it will be death to talk of it.

There is a great difference between presumption and full assurance. Full assurance is reasonable: it is based on solid ground. Presumption takes for granted, and with brazen face pronounces that to be its own to which it has no right whatever.

Beware, I pray you, of presuming that you are saved. If with your heart you do trust in Jesus, then are you saved; but if you merely say, "I trust in Jesus," it does not save you. If your heart is renewed, if you shall hate the things that you did once love, and love the things that you did once hate; if you have really repented; if there is a thorough change of mind in you; if you be born again, then have you reason to rejoice. But if there is no vital change, no inward godliness; if there is no love to God, no prayer, no work of the Holy Spirit, then your saying, "I am saved," is but your own assertion, and it may delude, but it will not deliver you. Our prayer ought to be...

"Oh that you would bless me indeed, with real faith, with real salvation, with the trust in Jesus that is the essential of faith; not with the conceit that begets credulity. God preserve us from imaginary blessings!"

I have met with people who said, "I believe I am saved, because I dreamed it." Or, "Because I had a text of Scripture that applied to my own case. Such and such a good man said so and so in his sermon." Or, "Because I took to weeping and was excited, and felt as I never felt before." Ah! but nothing will stand the trial but this, "Do you abjure all confidence in everything but the finished work of Jesus, and do you come to Christ to be reconciled in him to God?" If you do not, your dreams, and visions, and fancies, are but dreams, and visions, and fancies, and will not serve your turn when most you need them. Ask the Lord to bless you indeed, for of that sterling verity in all your walk and talk there is a great scarcity.

Imaginary blessings to the saved

Too much I am afraid, that even those who are saved; saved for time and eternity; need this caution, and have good cause to pray this prayer that they may learn to make a distinction between some things which they think to be spiritual blessings, and others which are blessings indeed. Let me show you what I mean.

Answered Prayer— Is it certainly a blessing to get an answer to your prayer after your own mind? I always like to qualify my most earnest prayer with, "Not as I will, but as you will." Not only ought I to do it, but I would like to do it, because otherwise I might ask for something which it would be dangerous for me to receive. God might give it me in anger, and I might find little sweetness in the grant, but much soreness in the grief it caused me. You remember how Israel of old asked for flesh, and God gave them quails; but while the meat was yet in their mouths the wrath of God came upon them. Ask for the meat, if you like, but always put in this: "Lord, if this is not a real blessing, do not give it me." "Bless me indeed."

I hardly like to repeat the old story of the good woman whose son was ill; a little child near death's door; and she begged the minister, a Puritan, to pray for its life. He did pray very earnestly, but he put in, "If it be your will, save this child." The woman said, "I cannot bear that: I must have you pray that the child shall live. Do not put in any ifs or buts." "Woman," said the minister, "it may be you will live to rue the day that ever you wished to set your will up against God's will." Twenty years afterwards, she was carried away in a fainting fit from under Tyburn gallows-tree, where that son was put to death as a felon. Although she had lived to see her child grow up to be a man, it would have been infinitely better for her had the child died, and infinitely wiser had she left it to God's will.

Do not be quite so sure that what you think an answer to prayer is any proof of divine love. It may leave much room for you to seek unto the Lord, saying, "Oh that you would blessed me indeed!"

Exhilaration of spirit— So sometimes great exhilaration of spirit, liveliness of heart, even though it be religious joy, may not always be a blessing. We delight in it, and oh, sometimes when we have had gatherings for prayer here, the fire has burned, and our souls have glowed! We felt at the time how we could sing—
"My willing soul would stay
In such a frame as this,
And sit and sing herself away
To everlasting bliss."
 So far as that was a blessing we are thankful for it; but I should not like to set such seasons up, as if my enjoyments were the main token of God's favor; or as if they were the chief signs of his blessing.
 Perhaps it would be a greater blessing to me to be broken in spirit, and laid low before the Lord at the present time. When you ask for the highest joy, and pray to be on the mountain with Christ, remember it may be as much a blessing; yes, a blessing indeed to be brought into the Valley of Humiliation, to be laid very low, and constrained to cry out in anguish, "Lord, save, or I perish!"
"If today he deigns to bless us
With a sense of pardoned sin,
He tomorrow may distress us,
Make us feel the plague within,
All to make us
Sick of self, and fond of him."
 These variable experiences of ours may be blessings indeed to us, when, had we been always rejoicing, we might have been like Moab, settled on our lees, and not emptied from vessel to vessel. It fares ill with those who have no changes; they fear not God.

Calmness — Have we not, dear friends, sometimes envied those people that are always calm and unruffled, and are never perturbed in mind? Well, there are Christians whose evenness of temper deserves to be emulated. And as for that calm repose, that unwavering assurance which comes from the Spirit of God, it is a very delightful attainment; but I am not sure that we ought to envy anybody's lot because it is more tranquil or less exposed to storm and tempest than our own.

There is a danger of saying, "Peace, peace," where there is no peace(Jer. 6:14), and there is a calmness which arises from callousness. Dupes there are who deceive their own souls. "They have no doubts," they say, but it is because they have little heart searching. They have no anxieties, because they have not much enterprise or many pursuits to stir them up. Or it may be they have no pains, because they have no life. Better go to heaven, halt and maimed, than go marching on in confidence down to hell. "Oh that you would bless me indeed!"

My God, I will envy no one of his gifts or his graces, much less of his inward mood or his outward circumstances, if only you will "bless me indeed." I would not be comforted unless you comfort me, nor have any peace but Christ my peace, nor any rest but the rest which comes from the sweet savor of the sacrifice of Christ. Christ shall be all in all, and none shall be anything to me except himself.

O that we might always feel that we are not to judge as to the manner of the blessing, but must leave it with God to give us what we would have, not the imaginary blessing, the superficial and apparent blessing, but the blessing indeed!

Our work and service— Equally too with regard to our work and service, I think our prayer should always be, "Oh that you would bless me indeed!" It is lamentable to see the work of some good men, though it is not ours to judge them, how very pretentious, but how very unreal it is. It is really shocking to think how some men pretend to build up a church in the course of two or three evenings. They will report, in the corner of the newspapers, that there were forty-three people convinced of sin, and forty-six justified, and sometimes thirty-eight sanctified; I do not know what besides of wonderful statistics they give as to all that is accomplished. I have observed congregations that have been speedily gathered together, and great additions have been made to the church all of a sudden.

And what has become of them? Where are those churches at the present moment? The dreariest deserts in Christendom are those places that were fertilized by the fertilizer of certain revivalists. The whole church seemed to have spent its strength in one rush and effort after something, and it ended in nothing at all. They built their wooden house, and piled up the hay, and made a stubble spire that seemed to reach the heavens, and there fell one spark, and all went away in smoke; and he that came to labor next time; the successor of the great builder; had to get the ashes swept away before he could do any good. The prayer of every one that serves God should be, "Oh that you would bless me indeed." Plod on, plod on. If I only build one piece of masonry in my life, and nothing more, if it be gold, silver, or precious stones, it is a good deal for a man to do; of such precious stuff as that, to build even one little corner which will not show, is a worthy service. It will not be much talked of, but it will last. There is the point: it will last.

"Establish the work of our hands upon us; yes, the work of our hands establish it."(Psalm 90:17). If we are not builders in an established church, it is of little use to try at all. What God establishes will stand, but what men build without his establishment will certainly come to nothing.

"Oh that you would bless me indeed!" Sunday-school teacher, be this your prayer. Tract distributor, local preacher, whatever you may be, dear brother or sister, whatever your form of service, do ask the Lord that you may not be one of those plaster builders using sham substances that only requires a certain amount of frost and weather to make it crumble to pieces. Be it yours, if you cannot build a cathedral, to build at least one part of the marvelous temple that God is piling for eternity, which will outlast the stars.

CHAPTER 4
God's True Spiritual Blessings

I have one thing more to mention before I bring this sermon to a close. The blessings of God's grace are blessings indeed, which in right earnest we ought to seek after. By these marks shall you know them.

Blessings indeed, are such blessings as come from the pierced hand; blessings that come from Calvary's bloody tree, streaming from the Savior's wounded side; your pardon, your acceptance, your spiritual life: the bread that is food indeed, the blood that is drink indeed; your oneness to Christ, and all that comes of it; these are blessings indeed.

Any blessing that comes as the result of the Spirit's work in your soul is a blessing indeed. Though it humble you, though it strip you, though it kill you, it is a blessing indeed. Though the harrow go over and over your soul, and the deep plough cut into your very heart; though you be maimed and wounded, and left for dead, yet if the Spirit of God does it, it is a blessing indeed. If he convinces you "of sin, of righteousness, and of judgment" (John 16:8), even though you have not hitherto been brought to Christ, it is a blessing indeed. Anything that he does, accept it; do not be dubious of it; but pray that he may continue his blessed operations in your soul.

Whatever leads you to God is in like manner a blessing indeed. Riches may not do it. There may be a golden wall between you and God. Health will not do it: even the strength and marrow of your bones may keep you at a distance from your God. But anything that draws you nearer to him is a blessing indeed. What though it be a cross that raises you? yet if it raise you to God it shall be a blessing indeed.

Anything that reaches into eternity, with a preparation for the world to come, anything that we can carry across the river, the holy joy that is to blossom in those fields beyond the swelling flood, the pure cloudless love of the brotherhood which is to be the atmosphere of truth forever; anything of this kind that has the eternal, immutable mark is a blessing indeed.

And anything which helps me to glorify God is a blessing indeed. If I be sick, and that helps me to praise him, it is a blessing indeed. If I be poor, and I can serve him better in poverty than in wealth, it is a blessing indeed. If I be in contempt, I will rejoice in that day and leap for joy, if it be for Christ's sake; it is a blessing indeed. Yes, my faith shakes off the disguise, snatches the vigor from the fair forehead of the blessing, and "counts it all joy"(James 1:2) to fall into diverse trials for the sake of Jesus and the recompense of reward that he has promised. "Oh that we may be blessed indeed!"

CHAPTER 5
Practical Application

Now, I send you away with these three words:

"Search." See whether your blessings are blessings indeed, and be not satisfied unless you know that they are of God, tokens of his grace, and pledges of his saving purpose.

"Weigh," that shall be the next word. Whatever you have, weigh it in the scale, and ascertain if it be a blessing indeed, conferring such grace upon you as causes you to abound in love, and to abound in every good word and work.

And lastly, *"Pray."* So pray that this prayer may mingle with all your prayers, that whatever God grants or whatever he withholds you may be blessed indeed. Is it a joy-time with you? O that Christ may mellow your joy, and prevent the intoxication of earthly blessedness from leading you aside from close walking with him! In the night of sorrow, pray that he will bless you indeed, lest the wormwood also intoxicate you and make you drunk, lest your afflictions should make you think hardly of him. Pray for the blessing, which having, you are rich to all the intents of bliss, or which lacking, you are poor and destitute, though plenty fill your store. "If your presence go not with me, carry us not up hence." (Exod. 33:15).

But... "Oh that you would bless me indeed!"

Made in the USA
Las Vegas, NV
16 January 2022

41491076R00015